Title:Manners my Grandma taught me

Author: Purpose Copeland

Illustrated by: Michael Clemons (Teddy Graphics)

Publisher: Black Authors Rock, LLC

For information address Black Authors Rock www.BlackAuthorsRock.com

ISBN: 978-1-947970-12-0

http://www.everyonespurpose.com/

For booking inquiries email LaTracey@BlackAuthorsRock.com

Purpose Copeland is an 8 year old who loves life and everyone in it.
She believes that she is Everyone's Purpose until they can figure theirs out on their own.
She loves art, dance, drama and traveling.
She currently is being homeschooled with an entrepreneurial track.
Her business, Everyone's Purpose, teaches about the importance
of loving yourself with self-care products and activities.
Purpose is blessed to have an abundance of family that love her!

Everyone's Purpose

PRESENTS

Manners My Grandma Taught Me

By: Purpose Copeland

Hi my name is Purpose!

Everyone's Purpose is different but we all have one!

Purpose is your gift from God.

Destiny is your gift back to Him.

Let's explore the purpose my grandma has in my life

Dedicated to all that love me!

My grandma taught me about God

To respect the church, pray and praise God for myself.

My grandma taught me to be kind to others!

Don't point your fingers at them!

My grandma taught me to sit like a lady.

My grandma taught me to stand up for what I believe in!

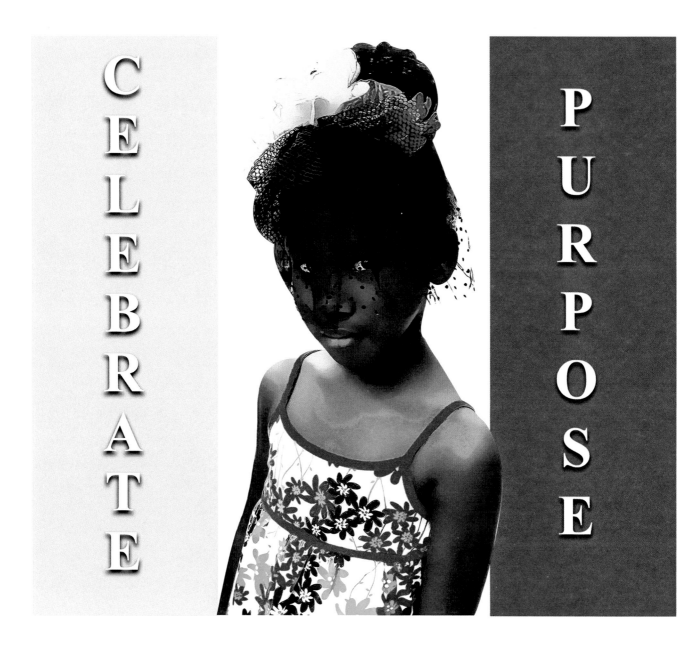

CELEBRATE PURPOSE

My grandma taught me to celebrate myself.

**R
E
S
P
E
C
T**

My grandma taught me to look people in the eyes!

Q
u
e
s
t
i
o
n
s

My grandma taught me it's okay to ask questions!

**My grandma taught me to use my inside voice!
No yelling at them!**

**My grandma taught me to be "the woman"!
Dressing cute is important!**

My grandma taught me to a stop and smell the flowers
and appreciate the little things.

When asking for something, say "Please and Thank you!"

When talking to adults, say
"yes ma'am and no ma'am or yes sir and no sir!"

Say "excuse me" when grown ups are talking!

SPEAK. Always introduce yourself to adults
who come visit, and introduce friends to each other.

Wash your hands! You already know about Coronavirus!

My Grandma Taught Me Manners Are Important

The End

10924629R00015